W9-BSF-160

MY VENICE

Harold Brodkey

My Venice

METROPOLITAN BOOKS
HENRY HOLT AND COMPANY
New York

Metropolitan Books
Henry Holt and Company, Inc.
Publishers since 1866
115 West 18th Street
New York, New York 10011

Metropolitan Books™ is an imprint of
Henry Holt and Company, Inc.

Copyright © 1998 by Ellen Brodkey
All rights reserved.
Published in Canada by Fitzhenry & Whiteside Ltd.
195 Allstate Parkway, Markham, Ontario L3R 4T8

Originally published in German translation in 1997
under the title *Venedig* by Rowholt Verlag.

Owing to limitations of space, permission to reprint previously
published material may be found on page 115.

LIBRARY OF CONGRESS CATALOGING-IN-PUBLICATION DATA
Brodkey, Harold.
My Venice / Harold Brodkey.—1st ed.
p.   cm.
ISBN 0-8050-4833-2 (hardbound : alk. paper)
1. Venice (Italy)—History—Fiction.   I. Title.
PS3552.R6224M9   1998   97-28899
                                                        CIP

Henry Holt books are available for special promotions and
premiums. For details contact: Director, Special Markets.

First American Edition 1998
Designed by Kathryn Parise

Printed in the United States of America
All first editions are printed on acid-free paper. ∞

1   3   5   7   9   10   8   6   4   2

CONTENTS

MY VENICE

Approaches

The airplane's course from Rome to Venice—a long crosswise swirl and then a spike going north with a small half-circle at the end—went from side to side of the peninsula from the Tyrrhenian to the Adriatic and up half the length of the boot of Italy past Ravenna and Ferrara to the foot of the Alps.

At one point, the plane banking over the Adriatic in clear air was suspended over the dimpling and restless glare of the sea, one sun-washed section of which was a dancing, unpictorial, pallidly gold mosaic, unimaginably far below.

All in all, the ancient ages and the Gothic moment and the *Rinascimento,* all the historical past, whispered briefly, foreshortened and terrifying below—the stone monuments and deaths—a moment of flight time here, a few seconds there—in the plane's ravenlike shadow. The flight lasted an hour, actually sixty-three minutes. It represented a new Italian meaning of eagles and gods, *dei ex machinarum* and angels-turned-demons spilled from the realized City of God and become air travelers in the wan hubris of vacationing or on business jaunts. Or returning to their childhoods.

My Italy now is a tangle of flight times, suburbs, superimposed cultures, a country caught up in affluent hysteria, modern but hoping that the modern was something that could be played at.

But the modern moment is unforgiving, no matter whether it is also unforgivable.

When the plane landed, the old-fashioned clock tick before quartz, or even medieval time animated by brute noise and church bells, seemed for a moment to have been restored and to rule still over footsteps and travelers and my life. We had returned to the other story, the other story still existed—or might resume—at any moment. But I realized soon that here too, even on earth, on dry land, time was modern.

On the motorboat I hired to bring me into Venice, where I had lived for a large part of my childhood and then again in adolescence, the heavyset boatman, the water chauffeur—dressed like Humphrey Bogart in *The African Queen*—opened up the engine, opened the

throttle when we came near the mouth of the airport
inlet, and the bow lifted; and we went skidding and
sliding thumpingly across the gray water of the lagoon
in the lane set out by new channel markers. And apartment complexes, factories, smokestacks, bridges, and
the chemical pall of terra firma were dimly visible
in the distance all around the shore of this part of
the lagoon in the gray light. A rainy, clouded afternoon with motionless, shroudlike light, weighted as
if by rain.

So, the story here too was of a new order, much as I
would have liked to be comfortably held by the old
description.

The motionless almost-stillness of the gray light is an
illusion. One knows the light is unstill, more unstill than
the boat or plane, more unseeably unstill than the mind
which broodingly *ticks* or sput-sputs and glides and
slimly speeds and flatters itself that the light of thought is
swifter and steadier than light itself. To be honest, one's
eyes, not as young as they had been, do see the raindrop-
clouded light as a haze of grayly luminous motions, see
this while my body is shaken by the mechanically solid
jazz of the motorboat engine and while I hear the not
entirely muffled noises of other engines in other boats
not far off from us in these channels.

And the whisking movements of the eyelids, and the
shift of images on the retina and in the mind, are part of
the web of restlessness in which one approaches Venice,

part of the variable and moist and tickling instantaneities of dimmed and jostling rhythms and emotions. . . . Here is the self and the hovering moment; here is the trembling, nervous, seemingly near motionlessness of the surface of the water; here is the rustling bow wave and wake; here they are in subduedly echoing canals in Murano; then here is the lagoon again, Venice ahead obscured; here is San Michele on the left pretending that the dead are silent and are not numberless; here is the gouging and choppy passage of the white motorboat over gray fluidities, the lighted grayish rain-teased air holding a glow as of a decomposing moon, and I am enveloped in flitters of memory, which I resist, of the canals in Venice itself, the wrinkled water in the *rio* behind our house, the secret hushes and whispers there, time's indescribable motion on a Venetian afternoon. I was a child here. And here is my history of love. I see eternity-in-reverse now, welling up as reality, a reality which is particularly Venetian and which is mine, no part of which is eternal, my Venetian reality in a modern moment.

It is a sense of time and of my own life on which my mind is sailing so wildly, time emerging from *the direction* of my father and moving in the direction of my death and bearing and containing my life.

The day brightens infinitesimally, and here is the Sacca della Misericordia, in which at once the motorboat slows and the bow comes down. To the left, quite high, are statues in the air, on the roof on top of the delicately subsiding fabric of the Gesuiti, stone versions of angels riding in wonderful absurdity and suggestive of belief in the gray-blue air—blue because it is brightening somewhat, only a little, but somewhat. In the damp air, in the pause in the rain, buildings here rise on either side in pink and worn rosy walls and terraces forming abrupt, closed-in, yet somehow grand perspectives. Proud Venice. When I was adolescent I woke sensually each morning nearly always as an experience of falling into this world. In the narrow Rio di Noale, the wind kept out and light obscured, the boat putt-putts in the shadow. At the end of the long open-roofed shadowed tunnel of this *rio* is a half-strongly lit, horizontal-but-as-if-tilted slab of wavery water in the Grand Canal, into which after a moment or two of heartbeat we ride. Which is to say, into the wider view we come.

And the motorboat slues and heaves in the bright, sharp chop of the Canalazzo, in a sudden unfurling of a broad reality of gray-lit water and tilted palaces. Really, it is like a gathered thought, the scene, half-worded, incompletely visible, greedy toward reality, to hold it, and full of a will to display itself, and beautiful.

The boatman let me off at Sant' Ortellia. The porter sent from the palazzo where I will stay waits with a two-wheeled hauler where he stows my suitcase and my briefcase and my notebook computer. I hurried ahead of him.

Now I move into the narrow shadow of the *calle* and I come at once into the shade of a number of fragments of memory, and then after a hundred yards or so to a narrow canal, the Rio Piotin, with water too low for the motorboat and with thin sheaves of somewhat brightish, somewhat yellowish light visible here and there among the walls. On the heavy, tossing silk of the unclean water, seabirds, white, and black-headed, beaked, float: small, living gondolas. Jiggling necklaces of light move on the damp lower walls of the palazzi. An ocean has been funneled into greenish mirrors among walls softly and narrowly lit like this. In this city much of the direction of my life was established.

In the cold shadow where I stand, I grin inwardly and move over the high-backed curve or stone curl of a *ponte storto*–distorted bridge—and I come to the Campo Marinention. I am giving it a fictional name. The old, many-windowed, double-loggia'd palazzo, handsomely bent and cleverly restored and so gently conceited and airy, bears the Venetian imprint, is an expression of the Venetian theme of secular grace. It has two trees in front of it, leaves fluttering in the wind, and a Renaissance wellhead; and part of the façade and the center of the *campo* is touched by a spread of clear light.

I gaze at the palazzo façade in the light. I move

toward the light, and my heart shifts its weight
when I pass into it, into the clear light—I feel myself
in Venice to be at home in the amoral grandiloquence
of the light.

(Profane Friendship)

One arrives, if one comes here often, sooner or later
in a moment of mist, mist on the water, a vapory
sky. . . . Then the rhythms of travel by train or car on
the causeway bear one along until what becomes visible, up to a point, are buildings among the vapors, a
few domes, a campanile or two, a large ship at anchor,
roofs—among the vapors which shift and which let
long Adriatic shafts of light appear as if from behind
a veil.

At a certain point, after a transition of crowds and
parking the car, one becomes aware of the absence of
wheeled traffic and of the lapping sounds of water, the
tongue and the lap, and memories, the sense of enormous wealth in a given early moment of childhood, a
garden and a dog, return.

Venice is not a city one associates with childhood. It is
mind and ferocity and amusements in a city water-
begotten as in a dream or in a story beneath the
immense Adriatic clouds in what was always a wilder
arm of Europe.

(Unpublished note)

I was returning to my old sense of things, to the place from which most of the settings and details of my dreams were derived.

Venice in the distance, across the water, neared as the train racketed on worn railroad ties on the causeway. The train, the causeway, everything needed repair. We expected nothing to work. It was early October, the middle of a school term, the middle of the day. Time has no geometry of middles. The moment of arrival is mist and damp warm air, a lingering and uneven warmth from the leftover summer, a dank coolness here and there, familiar buildings looking worn, and no sun. And in the sunlessness, the shiftingly dirty water in the smaller canals.

Venice lay in a fog, a mist. Among the shapes of the mist moved apparitions, the sounds of footsteps were brooding and spectral. . . .

Venetian dialect returned, almost an emanation of the buildings, an echo, or voices overheard, the shouts of gondoliers around a bend in a canal, the scutter of voices, then my voice.

And they, the buildings, began again, stone by stone, to be my old and new surroundings after their long sojourn in distorted forms in memory. Memory leaped, and reclothed itself so that in the span of gray, foggy days, the Salute and the Palazzo Labia, the Libreria, and the campanile of Santa Maria Formosa in their softly shrouded present forms were known to me as if I had

seen them all along without remission in sunlight,
clearly lit.

Shrouded, post-war Venice in the silvery gloom emerged prowlike, looming with accumulated emotion and beauty, an-ocean-liner-in-a-dream, but real, really my home. Everyone seems older and wiser after a war, for a moment or two, even me, but it seems each person is wiser in ways different from everyone else—there is an anarchy in the wisdoms, and empty places. In a sense, no one had been clearly instructed by the war—that nightmare teacher. . . .

In Venice daughters were nursing very old fathers for whom there was no structure of succor at the moment, the local men often somewhat catatonic, expartisans, stalked the right wing, the Fascist bureaucracy and soldiers and sailors who had returned were a whipped majority—what is charity now? The papers said *the nation must get on its feet,* but the joke in dialect was that the nation had only one foot. Italy shaped like a boot, has a single foot and is a nation-amputee. The nation hopped like a war grasshopper.

People without much power moved in the shrouded paucity of light, moved in the silvery drifting of the air, in the fog stained by the smoke from the city's innumerable coal stoves. At noon a yellow stain with burnt rainbow veinings of brownish tints discolored the fog over the glinting and shifting Canalazzo. Cloudy figures as high as the clock tower blew and swayed in the Piazza.

14   The haunted carnival of the aftermath of war wasn't a matter of peace and hope at last but of the reality of horror and life going on anyway, as if concussed and distracted by what had happened. Or empty. Some human abdication in modesty and disorder left the days to be mostly a parade of the reality of time which was a kind of realism and of modesty, as I said.

(PF)

Two things I know about Venice. Nowhere in the city does the eye rest on a human claim to omnipotence and divine right. The jumble of culs-de-sac and sudden unfoldings into small and then large spaces and then curving or twisting, more or less outspread vistas with ultimate perspectives in them of lagoon and sky don't suggest a single kingly eye. And the haphazard bounding upward of the walkways onto the high-instepped footbridges over the rustling canals, bridges which block your forward view until you mount high enough on their steps, the crowd of unknown people around, all of them on foot—none of that suggests royal divinity. Nothing in Venice represents the rickety stuff of centralized kingly will, and the pious self-hypnosis of one person who is the living, hereditary embodiment of the entire place and of others who love the place (and their place in it) with a similar and lesser and less pious self-hypnosis of their own.

No. Here is an abrupt commercial canniness mixed with daydreaming and an unbelievable depth of having trafficked in daydreams commercially for centuries. That is the other thing I know about Venice.

(PF)

And: The Inquisition was never established in Venice. It was a shameless city of courtesans and of greed, bare-breasted Cleopatra on the wall.

(earlier draft)

I will tell you a fourth thing about Venice: it is not a city in which black has much meaning. Even the stains here are rarely black. And night rarely. Black plays little role in Venetian painting. Black as a color for clothes is Dutch and French, Spanish and English, but not Venetian. Black here is luminosity, is color lightly asleep, veiled.

(PF)

I have just found out something. If you are a person who asks if something is morally O.K., if you examine things to see their value now and in the future, if you do them—or if someone else does them—if you study and ask over and over, and are practical and if you learn, you are only a step away from that spirit of being a trader in a commercial Christian republic, one who deals in things of value and in wars. It is the basic training for commerce in the real world, a harried conscience. That is one of the secrets of Christian Venice and of the other trading republics, don't you agree? How a certain mercantile opportunism arises from the examination of conscience? First such serious citizens, fishermen, then Hamlets, then merchant princes and great fortunes.

(earlier draft)

If I were a *Herr dottore* I might suggest that it was neurally impossible to contemplate actuality, the continuous time in which we live. Perhaps with the help of outlines and thoughts on paper, we can glimpse it and run or bounce or carom from glimpse to glimpse. But the true story is lost to us in the errancy of memory which must inevitably shatter and fly about and run off like spray and water splashes from the stubbornness of the reality of continuous time.

I mean that one can only dive in, and not swim there, in the lost canals of an earlier moment, not swim continuously. Perhaps it is spiritually impossible to accept that Time *is* continuous, unbroken and of irresistible majesty. Perhaps one must have symbols whose motion can be altered and gainsaid and denied. One can deny God. But time, ah time, its direction is unyielding and

one cannot alter physically the physical dimensions of
a moment.

Venice sits among the waves and among the winds and the silent continuousness of time.

(PF)

Venice is a separate country. It cannot properly be part of Italy, or part of anything. It floats at anchor inside its own will, among its domes and campanili, independent and exotic at its heart, a collection of structures among the waters, monuments of independent will, a city of independent will.

In Venice, here on the vaporetto landing at Sant' Ortellia with the façades of palaces visible in an irregular line along the watery, water-carved curve of the Canalazzo, time seems to be illuminated in the moist air, an arriving moment is so immediate and obvious in its approach and in its reality as yet another moment of one's life. . . . This motion is exemplified in the faint, pale yellow appearing in the east and lying lightly in long rays on the façades and small waves and perceptibly changing moment by moment. Time is different here than on the mainland, in the cities or countryside there. Affection is untied to the departing moment and is perhaps not refastened unless you or events fasten it again, rebutton it. The boundless *medias res* in which we live, and the intermittences of attention when there is no pause of bodily reality—and our unawareness of the

18   basso continuo or ostinato of pulse—and our awareness
of the discontinuities of the mind's tenor and soprano
and baritone—explain why presence has its quality as
beauty for the mind's comfort and beyond it, to the
mind's dismay and sense of imprisonment—I mean
presence is fidelity and belongs to one's continuing
heartbeat and breath, and not to the disjunctures of
attention.

The light moves between the buildings and on the
buildings and tricklingly on water. Actual light and
actual dark is everywhere in sight. The world is real.

(PF)

In real time in a real Venice, in real light, I am waiting
on the bridge of the Scalzi. Venice, although it is a theater and now a theater of rendezvous, is *real,* or was
once, in the soft brushing, folding, and unfolding of a
present moment; and there are the tawny hues of sunlit
walls and dark-red tiled roofs as I stand on the high-
arched Scalzi with the great running actuality of the
Canalazzo below me, the unstable glitter of the water,
the absurd, water-walking, bow-dancing traffic in yellowy sunlight.

If I turn in a circle I see, identified, massive structures, a railroad station, two churches, one on each side
of the Grand Canal, a railroad hotel, and the sky and the
lagoon, domesticated here, intimate but not miniature,

and the present moment which you know by this, that in
it everything is improvised. . . . The world alters blink-
ingly. . . .

(PF)

   The colors of the scene are now green and blue and
yellow with spots of red and dashes of white. The railroad station, the two churches, on each side of the Grand
Canal. The traffic on the Canalazzo in that bright light
below us. The real actors here improvise their lines.

(earlier draft)

Walks, Boatrides

The gathering morning strengthens its hold on the city. I walk in a spilled, taut quality of emotion—in an architecture of light. The noises of the city had a special quality emerging in the absence of the scirocco. Owned and goaded by my life, I walked in a painted city through painted air in a created world.

The ordinary, real, and ludicrous world has a sweet stillness, Venice as a continuous canvas with only sad, trapped elements of motion in it. . . . It seemed that I alone lasted; everything and everyone else was brief, was condensed into fixed, clear meaning, and I was as alone in my continuousness as I had felt I was in earliest childhood. Do you understand me? Do you remember? The

22   daylit canvas blows and stirs, picture-tinted, a flag,
loosely curling and unwinding.

(PF)

The motor noise, the passersby on the *fondamenta,* a
tall tourist pausing to watch us . . . Now we putt-putt
carefully past the piled up palazzi and tenements, past a
shabby *squeri*. Already we are putt-putting too noisily,
too fast, along the Rio San Giovanni Laterano to the Rio
San Lorenzo, again a bit faster, past the Carpaccio
"Cave," the small *scuola* where St. George and the
dragon are on the wall across from St. Jerome, and past
the Greci and into the Bacino and into the widening
light. With sudden speed—into a further widening of the
light and the motor noise and with an uplifted bow and a
bow wave lacing splashingly from us.

The Grand Canal slides and slices to the right, the
drifting façades, window-ridden, curving with fantasy.
A sense of gold.

Past San Giorgio Maggiore and its mysterious mathe-
matics of reflection and of worked stone and the echo-
campanile, the smaller version, still enormous, of the
great one in the Piazza which is too new, too coarse.

Past the Giudecca, onto the lagoon toward Chioggia,
the wide emptiness. Bow wave and loud racheting
motor noise and the wooden hull of the boat pound-
ingly bumping and skipping along on the uneasily heaving, weedy, sloppily dirty, watery field of the lagoon. A

truant pair, naval in the wind, and the ever-widening
maritime emptiness and light.

(earlier draft)

The light brightens, becomes unendurable, we flee to the Zattere in the hot, damp, steamy, drying air and have complicated ice cream concoctions on one of the large floating rafts there while vaporetti putt-putted to the landing stage and rocked the raft, and steam rose from the waves. The air had a pearly residue of spume in it.

On the vaporetto: toward Mestre, the sky beyond the edge of the cloud mass is sharply yellow again. Nearer us, massed clouds ride above the lagoon.

The vaporetto slews and chugs and splashingly shoves its way. We disembark. The crowd on the Riva smells of rain and summer.

We board yet another vaporetto, a black one. . . . The boat goes grinding loudly and hypnotically and almost glidingly across the shadowed, placid Bacino under the massed clouds. The sunlight near Mestre strides swiftly over the water toward us changing the sullenly gleaming blue-green-black surface of the water to glare, and the well-ordered face of San Giorgio Maggiore in a gloomy half-light into a tall church with pilasters and cornices damply sunlit. Across the Bacino behind us the bright city is only half-bright, and has vaporous outlines. Half the sky above it is dark. But vaporous brightness rises from the receding domes of San Marco. The water in the Bacino is touched with stirring and streaming vapors. I feel tangled in bright, steamy, lightly churning vapors. . . . And around us on the water stirs the expanse of damp, vaporous light. Thin tendrils of mist are streaming and vanishing in our passage. I am choked with the blind Utopian-apocalypticism of my hope of sentimental happiness.

Now we are in very bright, very hot sunlight. A flood of poisonous heat is spread burningly over the fields of water of the Giudecca. The close-textured air was like muslin drawn taut in the wind and then loosening as the boat progressed in its course past the austere Redentore atop its tourist-dotted steps . . . on the bubbling fluster and liquid cries of the water toward the Zattere. The wind sluggishly whirred. The Venetian outdoors seemed to be an open window with a realer outdoors farther on behind the hot blowing weave of yellowy light. The nearby stroking and tickling bunching of coarse heat, the brushingly palpable, light-tortured, curtain-like air hurt the skin, the eyes. To the south, visible in the bright, almost twinkling, almost evilly hot sky, was the dark cloud mass, domed and gray-blue-black, of the rain over the Adriatic. My head in its bell of rigid bone was clanging in hot, whited bystanderhood, a moral posture, an emotional fastidiousness . . . a snobbery, a snobbish autonomy.

(PF)

What I know, what I understand a little of, is that what the mirror holds, what Venice, old and delicate as glass, reflects back to me is half-proven truth, is a willed, partly fanciful, very old reality. A bridge, a canal, silence, a *campo,* a flow of tourists, noon light—I walk in noon light, in the whirring butter of such light and think of friendship and ambition, Venice and money. One has friends, resources—modes of protection; this is, in part, what adulthood is.

But the methods and modes of protection one has are perhaps not good enough protection against some people. People negotiate their favors, not always, but usually; and then, in real life, negotiate further; they own you; they deal in you behind your back—or over your head—like slave traders, like Venetians.

I walked in the whirring light to the Frari and entered the enormous floating space and went to the sacristy and sat looking at the Bellini there. It is something I do in Venice—the Bellini, a Madonna with Child and four saints, is human but is superhuman a bit, or touched with grace; the light in it moves from the human to the saintly to the nobly, gently, quietly, even silently holy. It has a golden architecture or geometry, a certain sternness of love, but the sternness is more like a spine. Love is very clearly love in it.

I felt a certain stale frenzy of stilled hysteria locked inside me that the picture softened or ignored. As I said earlier, when you age, the number of comparisons lessen but the comparisons are more final, perhaps

26   more oppressive and tyrannical, older, younger, smarter, stupider. . . . And the comparisons move in the moments, propelled by will and by plotting, by scheming. How strong still, how rich, how mad, how sane, how bitter and howling inwardly or how stilled and catlike, how frightened, how ferocious, how warm still, with how many fresh words left in the anticipatory silence now advancing in the increasing loneliness and *genius* that death is and which is given to us as death begins to take possession of us. How much then does one love the truth?

(PF)

Watery Venice, sunlit and fragile and a wind-floored seabird's glide fill my eyesight at this promontory tip at the end of my strength . . . at the rim of the black flitter of unconsciousness. Fluttering waves and flags of black absence from consciousness, a sea of this laps at me. Distances become opaque, but the wind and the sun are whispering, and the distance lessens, and I see the moment again in the light.

The wind clung and pushed and whined in the passage. A Venetian friend, naked-faced in the lightening dark, looked around with darting eyes. We padded along the empty *fondamenta* of the Zattere, the Giudecca pale across the water, and in the paling sky, more and more brightly luminous, the yellow dawn came up. A broad band of glossily yellow brightness was in the sky to

the east. The dawn poured pink and gray and pale-
yellow light—Venetian pink—into the *calli*, hazy and
tinted.

(PF)

We pass San Rocco in the sunlight, *scuola* and *chiesa*
consecutively ignored. Visual information is so ar-
ranged, so disarranged that day that the planes, the surfaces and volumes of buildings and faces and of talk and
the skeleton of emotional meaning have more than a
dry plausibility as we walk. Actuality, somewhat under-
sized, in the real Venice has that spilled, taut quality, per-
ilous, of good pictures and frescoes, as if one might fall
through the air in them or be struck dumb by the argu-
ments of faith or secular pleasure in them, or numbed
by the beauty of the Virgin with her infant, imprisoned
forever in her grief, or in Christ's death, or in some
saint's stillness of rumination.

It is as if the painter sold his soul and did not have a
genuine life and has created this one, for which you
might want to give up your life to share in it. Or to steal it.
And the life he gave up became the life of the figures and
of the image and of the iconographies, as of holy time
and then of saints' time and then of ordinary people's
time, each time characterized by a kind of light and by
architecture, holy or real, and by a gravity of the face and
by a special air.

(earlier draft)

The airlessness of the heat near San Sebastiano continued on the open Zattere. So much of flesh-pink and sallow Venice was visible that one expected coolness. But in its watery setting, Venice, the churches visible, Redemption and St. George, the city's humor of piety and erotic and forceful *wit* spread out in the heat.

Along the water, the nifty jumble of pretty buildings march beside the water dance. Little that is visible is dull; nothing in the scene is awesome. . . . This half-abandoned circus of a city, this dead city, my Venice in its lovely fields of wetly clanging, sunlit water, such a ferocity of decoration and appetite for happiness, for a lastingness of emotion, such a long echo of complicities, such a businesslike regard and appetite for love . . .

Venice offers such a pretty suffocation of resentment, such a sweetness over its violence, that I, spiritually, gag on it . . . stupid, ancient, movie-oid Venice. . . .

(PF)

The continuous outer tale, the outermost tale, is one's life in Venice, among the jumble of painted buildings and water: what is here is meant to amuse.

This unfinished movie of a city, this dead city, our Venice in its ring of water and in the concentricities of the canals, the lunge toward happiness, the ordinary cruelties of people in a city: the great flat but leaping

water and glare, white, blazing, the light burden of spray
in the hot wind.

(earlier draft)

Fitful swathes of sunlight appear, and they shrink and widen in the wind, bird-bursts of light, frail, nervous in the rain. Then the light flutteringly unfolds like cloth into damp, fresh-breathed sunlight.

Pigeons in the dark, on the roofs and *altanas* and below in the Campiello coo, squabble, court one another. . . . Venice seemed to plunge in a burst of wind, to be a flight-torn, trembling city. . . . God . . . Imagine God drunken. . . .

(PF)

The day is gray now. Pigeons fluffingly flap softly on the stones as we scatter them in our pace. We walk stiff-faced in cooler and cooler wind among tourists until near the Salute the light grows grayer still in the false twilight of before rain, and Venice holds its profile outlined in dull luminescence against the darkening sky.

Pigeons coo and paddlingly flap overhead inside and outside the story of feelings. The light in showy Venetian display strengthens to a glossy yellow fire. But then, clouds pile up again; blue-gray shadows like glass or like a powder are in the air; my eyes move pigeonishly in the glowingly darkening light. The sky's peculiar quality of light and dark in this moment of upper wind and lower stillness evokes a sense of personality, and of affection. This *campo*, this asymmetrical corner of Venice, is abuzz in the warm dark of the approaching rain, the array of stones and windows and birds and bells and light and children calling and rain coming. . . .

(PF)

Pigeons whir, and reflected light brightens on the stones in the damply glowing air. The green-gold horses prance, and the wetted rose and worn pink and glassy yellows of the mosaics of the church and the flesh-pink Loggetta and the gray-white statues on the roof balusters of the Libreria against the parting clouds and the streaked whitened bluish gray of the Bacino, the dulled radiance of the water, its small movements, in the outspread, dim, fluttering fan of its distances, the spreading plain of travelers' water in the lagoon beyond the Giudecca, the various bits of ruin and of modern ugliness only slightly interfere with the grace of the scene, the movement into perspective of the lovely city in the damp air, beneath now whitening clouds. The water at the moment holds more light than the air does. Brightness seems to rise from the water higher and higher, a semi-radiance without color. In

the Piazza, the dully glowing films of water everywhere
on wet stones gleam and shine, a muted, pale aura delicately and steadily brightening—the satisfaction for
the eye and the mind at the sweetness in the success
of men's work here and nature's decorative and significant docility, this, as so often in the past, amazes
and calms.

(PF)

The bells of Venice rang in the moist air as I blink-
ingly came to the door of the *altana*. I held myself
upright there. The sky bends down in narrow points
among the roofs and bell towers. There is a full moon
and small moon-whitened clouds. The first clanging
from distant and hidden bell towers is muted, partly
blocked by intervening buildings along the winding
calli. But then the bells from the visible towers start
up, San Stefano and the Frari and San Marco and its
Marangon, unleashing a loud, urgent, nearer clangor
mingling with the muted other clanging, filling the tight
fist of the city with arhythmic clamor. Around us, in the
dark city, above a few lit, pale façades, stone figures
stood and blessed or stared in the high, dark air—angels,
the Virgin, the evangelists, a few Christs—a stone population among the jumbled roofs, some with bronze
wings and bronze trumpets and bronze haloes in the
dark air.

(PF)

32   There are few representations of the Holy Ghost, the Holy Spirit, in Venetian art. In Venetian painting, angels and expressions on realistic faces suggest the *depths* of spirit.

(earlier draft)

The Piazza at night with the church-cathedral lit and the wind blowing the lights strung on guy wires high above the pavement, and a half-moon above the light with blowing clouds around it with moonlit, silver-gray, or bright silver edges in the dark blue, dark gray-black sky . . . And Florian's and Quadri's lit and an orchestra playing in front of Florian's, and girls everywhere, travel-stained or clean but pale with travel and with curious loneliness—floating in an oblique but vertically flowering sea of darkness, the surf of which was bits of light here, there, everywhere, up near the moon or floating on the pavement . . . The night is so many-surfaced that one could not fix a shape to it, and lamp- and moonlit in depthless and heightless constellations: the weird dimensionfulness of the night.

The darkness, adolescent nighttime in Venice, has in its shadows, girls. The mind remembering, remembers them as naked although it was the psychological and spiritual nakedness, the tourist simplicity in them because I was young, and it was the nakedness of their limbs and faces—their slender legs in the dark, the thinness of their clothes. Or it is some simplicity in how I see them, the elaborate fruit—forgive me—of darkness, of summer nights, and of our moods. Such girls grow into reality in the branches of darkness, tall, proud American girls, acquisitive and inquisitive, assertive French girls, too cruel, too intricate not to love and fear, and German or Scandinavian girls, gleamingly pallid, with skin the color of bones in the darkness, and English and Italian girls, shiny and dark or glistening and a bit rosy, conceited, knowledgeable, with young voices, and almost always with a noticeably foreign smell, a touch salty, and with an odd music, delicately unlinked, broken by travel—unless as sometimes happened they talked and would let no one else talk—how tough and boastful they sometimes were.

(PF)

Venice shabbily glittered in its beauty here and there in the airy, watery-floored perspective along the length of the Giudecca. Desire in me was like water splashing and overflowing a cupped hand, usable sloppily, but only wildly. . . . Nature created us as trespassers . . .

I blink and turn my head stilly toward the open water. . . . Past two gulls standing on the *fondamenta,* the water dances in the great arson and streaming flood of afternoon light. The upward swift motion of the seabird against the hot wind into the blasting light is like a fluttering sketch of a gondola. The bird briefly is alight, the stammering tines of metal atop the neck of the craft of its own flight. . . .

The gloriously yellow and clothlike and rippling sky that rose behind the dome of the Salute and its stone population of figures high in the air now rises still more brightly above the doubled row of palaces and the doubled and erratic reflections. Far inside me the sounds of the canal are ventriloquial, are spoken on the stage of darkness in me by my pulse, my breath, which are dream-thick, and which my mind parts like curtains, and I blearily stare through, while the gondola, rocking on the wavelets, is poled by the tall, red-faced gondolier into the light.

I have never seen such glitter—in the light on the waves and on the prow of the gondola and caught in the feathers of swooping seabirds and tonelessly exploding and adhering to the windows of the palazzi alongside us. Up the curved road of water and in the air lay the fancifully buzzing explosion of actual sun into the heat in which we advanced blindedly and rockingly. I ache with helplessness, with the return to being a child. As in childhood, I am beyond fright.

Now we are in dark green shadow.

(PF)

Sunlight brightly fluttered on glinting water and on faded, famous buildings as we putt-putted into the Canalazzo. The Salute, with its great dome of announce-

ment and its airborne, motion-struck population of
statues, gleamed in unreliable beauty, fabled unstone-
likeness. In the middle of the Grand Canal, a flotilla of
gondolas filled with Japanese surrounds a gondola with
an Italian tenor in it singing mostly on-key . . . A battered vaporetto laden with becamera'd tourists, red and
beset, startled and numbed in their staring, avoids the
Japanese.

(PF)

One time watching fireworks on the water here, I
imagined the mosaics of saints and the Virgin and of
Christ in San Marco become, in a sense, fireworks in
Venice burning and cascading and falling into the
Bacino. A far-off sizzle was audible in pauses of the
booming overhead, the extinguishing of the light.

(PF)

Tintoretto, the sad one, hardly painted the light of
Venice; he painted the light of the soul as moonlight or
as the light of metaphysical meaning.

(earlier draft)

On the Waves

In the churning wake of a motorboat from one of the luxury hotels, the gondola bobbed with graceful disequilibrium. The tall, thin, handsome man sitting in the gondola gripped the sides of the small wooden craft and said to his seven-year-old daughter, "Hold on." He thought, Gondolas are atavistic.

He wore a white polo shirt. Once he had been the sixth-ranking tennis player in the United States, and had married a rich girl; his days on the tennis circuit were five years past, and the marriage had ended in divorce twelve months before. Now he taught American history in an American school in Rome and played tennis with various members of the diplomatic set. He still kept to the course of reading he had drawn up and that he hoped would give him intelligence, or, failing that, education. Gifted with a strong body and good nerves, he had never felt so harassed by ignorance that a sense of his own worth could not come to his rescue; then in the fourth year of his marriage, his tennis game and marriage deteriorating, he had begun wanting desperately to know more about everything. He had settled down to read the philosophers, the psychologists, the historians, the poets, the critics. He had had no clear idea what he would do as an educated man, a self-made intellectual, and so he decided to teach. He had left his wife, unwilling to quarrel with her, unable to bear her restlessness at the change in him. He had gone to Europe. The divorce had depressed him. He had missed his daughter unconscionably. He wrote his former wife and asked if the child Melinda could visit him. He would pay her plane passage to Europe. His former wife agreed to permit the journey. Melinda had sent him a note in block capitals: "CAN WE SEE VENICE DADDY?"

She sat beside him in the gondola, white-skinned, thin-boned, with straight eyebrows like his and green eyes like her mother's. Her reddish-blond hair was her own. So was the dull stubbornness with which she maintained a polite and lifeless manner toward Henry. This was the fourth day of her visit, their second day in Venice.

He had a headache. He sat slouching, hands between his knees. He wondered irritably how the Venetians

managed to live day after day with the illusive and
watery haze, the heat, the mind-scattering profusion of
reflections, of smells, of playful architectural details,
with the unsettling mixture of squalor and ostentation,
with the silent, silvery air, the decay, the history, and the
atmosphere of vice. But he felt constrained to be honest.
The truth was, he thought ashamedly, he was bored. It
was dull as hell to spend so many hours in the company
of a child.

They had been to the Ca' d'Oro that morning. Henry
had said, "Isn't it pretty? It's supposed to be one of the
prettiest houses in Europe."

"It's pretty," the child said.

She had grown restless when he'd dawdled in front
of the Mantegna. "Tell me the story of that picture,
Daddy," she'd said.

"The man being shot with arrows is a saint," he'd said.

So much in Venice was unsuitable for a child.

It had been perhaps a mistake, this trip: movement
was half a child's charm. Children stilled—on a train, at a
dinner table, in a gondola—were reduced: one was
chafed by the limitations of their intellects and the hard-
ness of their voices.

When they'd left the Ca' d'Oro, they'd hired a gondola and embarked on the Grand Canal. Noticing the
child's lackluster eyes, the loose setting of her lips,
Henry had asked her, "You're not seasick or anything?"
He suggested, "Some people don't like gondolas. If the
gondola bothers you, we can go ashore."

"Could we have lunch?"

"I forgot," Henry had said. "It's your lunchtime. Can you hold out until we get to San Marco? I know the restaurants there."

As the gondolier resumed his steady stroke, Melinda turned to Henry—the angle of her head upon her shoulders indicated melancholy—and asked in a weak voice, "Why did they build Venice on the water?"

Henry replied without thought, "To be safe."

"It's safe on the water?"

Henry, whose eleventh-grade history students adored him and trusted his opinions, said, "Well, children might fall in. But the people here wanted to be safe from armies."

The child waited questioningly.

Henry was thinking that a gondola was an inefficient watercraft, keelless (a bent demiquaver, a notation of the music of the water). He woke from his reverie with a start. "Armies can't fight and swim at the same time."

"They could come in little boats," the child said.

Henry dusted off the knees of his trousers. "The Venetians could swim out and overturn little boats, they could do all sorts of things to little boats. The Venetians had no trouble with armies for a thousand years." He smiled to cover any deficiencies in his explanation—he had always been extraordinarily confident of his physical charm.

"A thousand years?" the child asked.

"Yes," he said reassuringly, "a thousand years."

The child closed one eye, looked at him through the other. "Is that a long time, Daddy?"

Henry swallowed a sigh. "I'll tell you," he said. "Let's take Grandmother Beecher. You think she's old, don't you?" Henry's eyes held the child's attention. "Now imagine *her* grandmother. And keep going back for *twenty* grandmothers. Isn't that a lot of grandmothers?"

His and the child's eyes seemed hopelessly locked. Then, as he watched, the child's eyes slowly went out of focus.

Slowly, she extended her arm over the water; she observed the shadow of her hand change shape on the sun-gilt waves. She was as lifeless as a mosaic, yet she spoke: "Are the palaces so wibbly-wobbly because they're so old?"

Henry said, "Well, yes and no." He paused, then went on heartily, "The buildings are old, yes, but that's not the entire story. The islands they are built on were mudbanks—they just barely stuck out of the water, and the Venetians made them bigger by throwing stones and logs and garbage—"

"Garbage—eeugh!" The child held her nose.

"Well," her father said, "they made the islands bigger. But as the years pass, the water licks away at them. Waves are like little tongues," he said with sudden poetry. "They eat out little pieces of the islands, the islands sink, and the buildings wobble." It was sad she was too young, Henry thought, for him to tell her that suns, stars, people, intelligence, and every other bit of created matter began by law in chaos and aged into chaos.

Melinda, squinting, peered up into Henry's face. "Is Venice falling apart, Daddy?" she asked.

"Well—yes and no," Henry said. "It's *sinking,* but very slowly."

"Gee, Daddy, you know an awful lot," she said with despairing enthusiasm.

Henry felt his face heating into a blush. He said, "Any guidebook would tell you . . ." He did not finish. He gazed at the Baroque palaces along this newer stretch of the Grand Canal, palaces spotted with noon shadows, draped in cornices, pilasters, and balustrades, sad.

"It won't fall down while we're here?" the child asked. She laughed faintly.

Did she want Venice to fall? Henry said, "No. It won't fall." It was disappointment he saw in her face. He said, "You know that big tower in the Piazza—the red tower? It fell down once. . . . In Henry James's time. About sixty years ago." Melinda was watching him, he thought, expectantly. She wanted to hear more about the collapse of Venice. Good God, why did the child wish harm to this fanciful city built on mud and garbage? Was it that, betrayed, she resented the world of adults, hoped for its destruction? Henry's heart trembled: the child was a betrayed idealist. Achingly, he looked at her.

She wore the dim frown that suggested she might be grappling with a half-formulated female thought.

"What is it?" Henry asked. "Are you thinking something? What are you thinking?"

The child, startled, shook her head and drew her shoulders up.

"You can tell me," Henry said encouragingly.

"You'll get angry," she said.

"Me?" He stopped. He said slowly, "It doesn't matter if I get angry. Fathers and daughters can get mad at each other if they want. It doesn't mean a thing. We can't go through life being afraid of each other." Melinda studied her thumb. "Why, if I got angry, I might shout and wave my arms and fall into the Grand Canal—wouldn't that be funny?"

Melinda was silent.

"Go ahead," Henry said. He leaned closer. "Try to make me angry. See what happens."

"I'm too scared."

"Of me?"

"I don't know," she said tactfully. She stuck her forefinger into the water. Henry could see only the back of her head.

He felt the rush of innocence that accompanies a sense of being misunderstood. "The water's dirty!" he exclaimed.

Melinda raised her finger and held it in her other hand on her lap; drops of water darkened her pale-blue skirt.

Henry said, "I don't see that anything you can tell me would make me any angrier than I am at your *not* telling me."

Melinda whispered, "All right. . . ." The gondola rocked. A lifeboat-shaped motor vessel was chugging by, stacked with Coca-Cola cartons. "I don't really like Venice."

He had expected her to say—his hopes had grown so from the moment when he realized she wanted Venice to fall—something more illuminating, something like an admission that it saddened her, the distance that had come between her and Henry since the divorce, something like "I hate it that you and Mommy don't live together anymore," something honest like that.

He said, "You wanted to come to Venice! It was your idea!"

"It's not the way I thought it would be," she said. "Nothing here is sincere except the water."

Henry's mouth opened, then emitted laughter. He laughed rather a long time. He sobered: Would Melinda care that a city was *insincere* if Henry's leaving home had not taught her that insincerity was everywhere? He blinked at her pityingly, tenderly.

"Why did you laugh?" Her face was pink with hurt.

"Because I thought what you said was witty." He watched her. "Do you know what 'witty' means?"

"No."

"Something true—more or less—that comes as a surprise and makes people laugh. That's witty."

"I did?" she said.

"Yes. You did. . . . But, Melinda, Venice is supposed to be nice, even though it's insincere," Henry said.

The child's face caved in, as if she took what he'd said for an expression of disapproval.

Henry, with that sensation of clumsiness that came to him whenever she asked him to help with one of her small buttons, tried to put things right. "But you like the water?"

"And the pigeons," the child said, anxious to please.

"Why? Are they sincere?"

"Yes," the child said, and nodded vigorously.

Why did she look so expectant? *I give up,* Henry thought, and laughed with exasperation and weariness. Melinda's face pinkened again, slowly. She smoothed her skirt. She seemed to have come into possession of a gentle incandescence. He said, "We certainly won't stay here if you don't like it. We can go to Paris."

"Paris?" The incandescence grew, then dimmed. "If you want to," she said, staring into her lap.

Henry had come to hate her pale good manners. The first days of her visit, he had thought she was still shocked that Mother-and-Daddy were no longer a single, hyphenated warm beast; he had told himself, "She will have to get used to me as an individual." He had not expected her to go on so long being mannerly and frightened with that individual. He began to rattle off words like a salesman trying to confuse a customer. "We'll go swimming—at the Lido—this afternoon. We'll take the launch over. We'll swim in the 'sincere' water, and tonight we'll eat and pack and have some ice cream, and tomorrow we'll fly to Paris. We'll fly over the Alps. You'll see the Alps—you've never seen the Alps before. We'll get to Paris in time for lunch. We'll have lunch outside on the street—"

"I know. I saw it on television."

"But you'll like it?"

The child said worriedly, "Do you have enough money?"

Oh, my God, Henry thought, *she did overhear those quarrels.* "No," he said, "I can't afford it. But we're going to do it anyway."

Melinda's eyes grew large. Her face seemed distended with pleasure. She put her hand to her mouth and laughed in the shelter of her hand.

Henry said, "What's so funny?"

"You're funny, Daddy. You're so bad." She inserted her hand inside his and gripped his fingers with an industrious and rubbery pressure—an active possession. Light dipped and danced along the swan's neck of the gondola's fantastic prow. She sighed. "Daddy," she said after a while. "You know that boy who lives across the hall?" From the apartment in the States where she lived with her mother, she meant. "Well, he likes to play dirty games."

Henry's tongue moved over his lower lip. He thought, *How strangely moving it is that the child trusts me.* "He does?" he said.

"Yes," she said.

"What do you mean by dirty games?" His eyes probed a corner of the Venetian sky; his voice was as calm as a psychiatrist's.

"You know."

"Give me an example."

"Oh, he wants me to go into the closet with him and take my clothes off."

The gondola slid under the Ponte dell'Accademia. Henry said, "Is that so?"

Melinda said, "Yes," nodding.

Henry switched his eyes to a different corner of the sky. "Is that all?" he asked.

"He's really silly," she said, noncommittal. ". . . He likes to push stomachs."

Henry heard the muted rumble of footsteps on the wooden bridge. "Do you like to push stomachs?"

Melinda said, "Sometimes." She drew the end of a strand of hair back from her cheek. "But I don't really like playing those games with *him*." She looked up at her father, her brows knit. "He gets angry if I won't play those games."

"Why does that bother you? What do you care if he gets angry?"

"Well, I don't like him to get too angry. I like having him to play with when I get bored."

"Is boredom so awful?" Henry said in a louder tone.

"It depends."

Henry thought, *She wants to punish me for abandon-*

ing her. My God. He made a mental note to do some reading about disturbed children. He said, shielding his eyes with his hand, "You stay out of that closet!"

A startled, single peal of involuntary laughter popped out of Melinda. She stared at him with pink astonishment.

"What's funny?" Henry asked.

"You are!" the child shouted. "What you're thinking! You want to kiss me!" Strands of hair bounced on her forehead in the silvery light. She spread her fingers over her mouth and cheeks, hiding them from him.

The sunlit panorama was squeezed into a rich oval in the center of which his daughter's face floated, partly veiled by her fingers. "You're right," Henry said, with amazement.

A flutter passed across the child's shoulders; a sound halfway between a choked shout and a laugh came from behind her fingers.

Along the canals, at the edge of his vision, Venice trembled on its uncertain islands, assailed by the devouring and protective and odorous wash of the sea. He kissed Melinda's hands, and as she moved them he kissed her cheek, her nose, her chin.

The gondola floated toward the seaward rim of the Piazzetta. Melinda's head lay on Henry's chest in the exhaustion following laughter. Her arm was thrown across his stomach. "We're at the Piazza," Henry said.

Melinda sat up, touched a hand to her hair. Groggily,
she surveyed the approaching landfall, the stone folds
of the perspective opening past the winged lion, the
lozenge-patterned palace, the benign litter of Byzantine
oddments, bronze horses, golden domes, pinnacles,
flagpoles, and pigeons. Amiably, the child said, "*Ciao,
piazza. Ciao,* lunch. *Ciao,* pigeons."

(Stories in an Almost Classical Mode)

The Unliterary City

Venetian art is not literary. It has never even been Bible-centered. The statue of St. Mark on San Marco, for instance, almost denies any ghostliness or idea or symbol: it is here and now. Too often, perhaps always, writing involves less emotion and drama, and less realism and feeling that can be checked against the real world, than was acceptable among Venetians. In all writing there is too strong a tendency to allegory, to the didacticism of outcome.

Money has always spoken for more in Venice than speech has. Money is a universal metaphor; it can be a metaphor for everything. It was that here—money and a private culture belonging to no one, and in need and fear of no one in particular. Worked stone and ships and water instead of books. Water is symmetrical in every direction, did you know that? Physicists tell us that. The realism of Venice brooked little in the way of allegory. It is almost as literal here as in Jerusalem. There, the real Mount Moriah, all of it is enclosed in the temple precincts. The whole mountain of Abraham and Isaac. In Jerusalem is the real Christ, not the Roman one who is Idea. (I read that Jerusalem was built on the summits of seven hills: an archipelago of summits.)

Venice is literal—real relics, real marble—and then fanciful because the literal erupts into error and Eros which are never *entirely* literal. Venice is entirely fact, and commercial fact but much of the commerce is in *How I Feel* and in *How I Look,* is like religious self-examination. Always enough realism to have no dictators. You see, only fantasy can imagine someone perfect or a situation so perfect that the person or the situation are deemed angelic or God-given or capable of rule.

Venice was never Utopian or apocalyptic. The United States is Utopian-apocalyptic, and this has become, since our founding, of great influence, among the French and then the Germans and then the Russians and then Marx and then the Fascists. Musso and Ezra. Venice never had the problems with alcoholism and drugs that absolute fantasies induce. Venice sought amusement and power and safety. I'll give you a silly image: it was like a great old actress of enormous vitality and cleverness and ruthlessness. . . . Venice is not a lonely place and not Utopia, and not apocalypse. That doubt of fantasy and of pretension, it militates against literature and the pomposity and daydreams of narrators and thinkers as well. Sometimes I think of Venice and the Venetians as having said to themselves, we must be realistic but reality is hard to bear; well, every chance we get we will dress it up; we will be realistic about fantasy and about the amusements of our inhabitants and we will survive.

(earlier draft)

Venice was never literary. It could not supply the necessary loneliness. And childhood's kingly hopes are dissipated here among the statues and the frescoes, angels and cherubs, spies and clowns, pantaloons and panders. And among the myths of dutiful heroes. The rich apparatus of emblems and elaborate façades spotted with carved heads and monsters at peace among the waters is a poetry self-consciously of fools and games.

An ambitious soldier and sailor had to go somewhere else to gain military glory and bring the news of it here, to the Rialto, where the local folk could make money from it.

I asked my father once why some book or other used the phrase *happy Venice*. And he chewed his lip and his at-that-time sloppy mustache, and he said that in his view Venice was a subtrahend, a batch of negatives—that is,

54   it was not grim, not stern, not-a-lot-of-those-things. . . .
And that added up to happiness or to something like it.
And I remember this very clearly—he said that no one
who was not Latin could understand.

(PF)

Old in Venice

One night during this time, after a dream of love, I woke and dressed and went out in the rain. *In Venice the rain was falling that day.* Rain in Venice wets the marbles of the cathedral and sets deep puddles in the pavement of the *calli*. And the canals sigh and ping. The noisy brightness of a rain with the sun half-emerged from Venetian clouds is like a noisy brightness of feeling, *la di da tra la la,* as in a comic opera of attachment and love with a happy ending, not as in a grand opera—that would be another story. A water rat, small and animate in the rain's mischievous light, runs along the edge of the Pescheria, a scuttering figure of animal wit. Workmen

are setting up the market. Trophies from the massacre of fish are piled on shiny beds of ice on tables under the roof in the open-sided structure. The fish at the end of their story, silver-bodied, with open red mouths and staring and unreal eyes, stink of brine, of the salt sea, stink of boats and are very still, gleaming, and limp.

The early morning's wet odors of rain, the smell of wet Venice, and the fish odor and the dirt and leaf smells of vegetables, and the drifting smell of gasoline fumes from the heavy workboats carrying food to the wharfside . . . the rainy smell of the Canalazzo and of dirt-marked hands . . . salt-odor and fish-blood-stained hands . . . The eyes and necks of the other lives here . . . The colors of faces and of stones in the rain . . . Me with my head erect in the rain under a gray umbrella, my remaining hair damp, my dry eyelids refreshed . . . I am a passerby in a fish market, gaudy-scaled, stinking, among the brown-tailed, sharp-finned fish, and the pale calamari and slow-stalking green *aragosti*. . . . In the rain, the carrots and tomatoes and apples and white celery and green cabbage are placed under paper, are loosely shielded from the light rain. . . . I am not clever. I am merely alive. Carlo Emilio Gadda has instructed my mood. . . . If he were here, he would perhaps understand me, my head suddenly lowered, ducking and staring at the stone paving underfoot to hide my tears, my rage, my embarrassment, my longing, my gratitude. I am riven with longing for that other world of feeling that no one has ever known, that other world of perfection, that world of pure and absolute love and of no appetite or heartbeat, of mouths that only sing. I am ill with longing—I who have not had a life of longing.

After a while, I lift my head, wipe my eyes, light a cigarette. . . . I rarely smoke but have begun to, lately. The bitter smoke, the match dry my eyes. The restless surface of the Canalazzo, wind-chopped, low waves seesawing and puckering in the damp air, is a few yards away past the edge of the stone wharf and the stacks of cartons and the lounging figures in rubber ponchos and stocking caps. The shadowed, restless air . . . now it is sputtering and spattering and spitting . . . Moisture stingingly touches my face, my present face. The sounds of drops on the umbrella and my faintly noisy breath under the fabric, the soft fabric-walled echo, and Venice, the Rialto, hurrying figures in the rain, outside the dripping scalloped rim of my umbrella . . . the busy, polluted rain and an aging man in a state of comic desire to know finally *what real love is* became, *finally,* a very strong, very unreasonable, very comic conviction that I was an example of it, perhaps not a good example, but love is so stupid, is so common, is so common a measure of life that anyone can be an example of it, even me, even if I am not the best example in the world.

In the rain-tinged air in Venice at the Rialto, the wind blowing and twisting the drumming umbrella, the hunger to feel love unchangingly and to be a person of fixed quality, fixed loyalty, fixed emotion, with assured

properties of trueheartedness and doting response
choked me.

Such peering as this at something in the light of truth—and of the spirit—was Christian. The spirit and the ordinary, perhaps grace-filled, perhaps tormented body . . . this peering was Venetian.

At the Riva del Carbon, in that crowded, cheap place, among the early tourists and the souvenir shops and nearby, the lineup of gondolas splashing among pilings, and the Rialto rising in the rain-streaked air, I thought how Venetian commercial speculation arose from a mind wandering during self-examination. Venice rising from the waves commercially was trained by the cate-chism in thought-out gambles of the soul and merchan-dise. Self-examination and modern capitalism have the same root.

(PF)

I went onto the loggia and into a scene of boats and sun-silvered, brightness-plated, blue-gray-green water, the Canalazzo in the last part of the afternoon. I was old, beset by age, and I saw tired, aging façades in glare, a concentrated shabbiness at the edge of a sun-gilded, filthy, immense ditch of water, but pretty enough. . . . Then the moment changes, and I am in Venice inside the watery surround, in this trembling city of age and fragility. And to be old in this old city is to have around one a visual music of great, spectral suitability. My memories of earlier conditions and even shapes of the buildings as I have known them are present as a frame for what is here in front of me. Such memories are insanely real, as real as what is here, but they go sliding into specterhood quickly, into ghostliness, into being lost presence like everything that has existed in this city until now, like all that has been lost; but the city in its dress of this moment moves more slowly in its own giddy continuities.

The eccentricity of Venice is that the facts of tragedy and of amusement here do not co-exist, not in story-dissolving Venice. A perverse sweetness is part of Venetian style, the absence of accusation and of lament, not always but mostly—the absence of lament along with an absence of coldness. So that one is warmly without lament—it is a style of being alive.

I said, "It is surprising to me how Venice has changed in color over the years. In my lifetime. The paint wears out. The stone darkens with dirt. And loses color as well. All of Venice has faded and been rebuilt brick by brick in my lifetime. I can date my life and identify the years in which I had certain feelings by the colors of the walls in my memory. . . ."

(PF)

This morning I woke at dawn, and the place announced itself immediately even in the near dark through the windows of my room, water and façades, moored boats, boats at work upon the glimmering surface of dark water. I wake nowadays once or twice before I wake. I often dream I am waking and feel the half-dark air and myself as real when it isn't yet the real world. . . . I'm not my age. I feel something like the silent clatter of my dreams, like horses on a shore, on the Lido, or the inland rim of the lagoon, horses and armed men, often Oriental, usually silent. I have discussed this with myself, who the silent Orientals are—perhaps Huns. I am mean, *hungry* after a night's sleep. But men of the East and not Lombards and the lumbering bombardment of the feudal wars of one's career, of one's politics. Goths and Vandals. Milanese. But Death. Or the dead. Or the barbarian young arriving in force during the night as Tartars and Mongols. And the sound of my own harsh breath is the snorting and clanging of war, of rage, left over from my night's dreams, from such invasion. Ruskin writes that Venice in the mid-nineteenth century was, at low tide, in the middle of a lagoon of mud, of seaweed and quaking, unstable muck. Desolation and uncrossability. There were miles of creeks and rills and wandering channels of deeper water which when the tide changed rose and overflowed among the seaplants and stirred them and made the mud of the higher knolls gleam, and then it covered all of it with its own shivering, reflectant symmetry, with reflections of the sky. Beauty arrives. The beauty of the city in the sea.

In the dream I had just before waking, I was rescued

from being hung on a gibbet in Cannaregio by masked figures, and then I fought in single combat like Sohrab and Rustum with my father or my brother Carlo on the edge of the lagoon, swords clanging on metal, eyes mad with quarreling, with nerves. The sky was deep red, maroon-vermilion, dark crimson, and purple, flames or sunset. And the dream, like most dreams, was shot through with emotion very clearly, with passion and fear, but this one was also full of contest and evidence of fatality, the fatality of close relationship.

Waking, I feel I have escaped from the rage and excitement, from the passionate focus and neatness of meaning or the dream.

(PF)

I grab at the day, at the fact of still being alive, today's fact of one's continuing existence—I truly wake only in stages attended by thoughts and perceptions. . . . City noises here resemble the sounds of breath, the sounds of someone in bed beside you, the sigh and *shuh* and creak of the mattress, the rustle of sheets, the clicking of eyelashes and the sough and slap of water, the flutter of wind, the clicking of footsteps in the *calle* . . . the sounds of familiar companionship mingling in peculiar neighborhood to one another.

Now that I am old—although people say kindly, hastily, *Oh you are not old*–I dress carefully always. I wear loose trousers, espadrilles in the old style, a thin sweater.

I was careful to check in the mirror that I had no mad, thoughtful look. I was not creased with mood or fright. I added dark glasses, a floppy hat; I had a semi-Italian public look.

I went downstairs into the *campo* and walked inland—I don't know why. It had something to do with a too-much-eyedness in me in my not being fully awake. Venice often seems to me to be inset with fluttering eyelids, the early wind, the half-light, the shuttered windows, the shuttered stores, and with what strikes me as the terrible wakefulness of the broad vistas of water, the murmuring wakefulness of the sea.

I walked in a direction opposite to the presentation of the naked idea of seamanship . . . The inanely entangled alleyways and high, humped bridges and stilled canals of sleeping-and-waking dawn-tinged inland island Venice represent clement shelter, a *tangled* clemency. One walks half-asleep in the empty *calli*. But ideas and sensations pick at one like the fact of the gaze, the *fluttering* eyelids of one's lover and her stare, waking one. Such unabstract sensations do literally seem like someone's living presence and gaze. So, in Venice, this least *Platonic* of cities, where for a millennium success had no conception of absolutes and was intelligent beyond any but physical description, one is ticklingly aroused by the ideas in the uncorrected sprawl and knot of streets and in the wandering façades of buildings matching the wandering paths of canals and of *calli*. Venice is human and eccentric, modified so little by touches of classical order that it seems to be free of any of the realities of modern absolutism.

Close by the Fenice, the Ateneo, so much handsomer before it was restored, so much lovelier before in its decayed, expensive Istrian stone, and curly cornices, is now stark white, and Scandinavian, and clearly outlined in cheaper stone and hastier workmanship than before. . . . The Scandinavians largely saved it. It has their mark, that cleanliness. But the stone is machine-cut and too slick now, lesser stone than before. The building's beauty is milder now in its modern incarnation. Light touches the stone figures atop it with their bronze fittings, the bronze trumpet, a bronze halo. In Venice I am at home in my own life—this ruffles my nervous, aging heart, and its emotional reflections of the physical morning that I have lived to see.

But *time* is where one truly lives anyway; a city is where one's self is moored for a time: Venice-in-a-given-moment. In boyhood, after school and its steady thoughts—its Platonism, its Thomism—I ran off into the hours here in the *calli,* as if into the bushes and woods elsewhere. Into the rushing flood and tide of momentary reflections, into boyish comparisons, faster or slower, funnier and less funny, taller or shorter . . . Strongly familied or out-of-luck . . . More frightened or less, more tumescent or less . . . More unreliable or less, often beaten at things or not lately beaten at things. I remember, and it is as if one were softly buffeted or teasingly beaten now too; some of the blows of memory are not jocular.

I know men who have become a little mad because they cannot escape the clutches of these comparisons. Fantasies about these comparisons abound, in movies, in sports and politics, in business, in cruelty, in love. For some women, the outcry is of the *perfect* . . . no more comparisons except in their favor, them being perfect.

The Piscine di Frezzaria is shadowed. Flowers bloom in a window box. Across a canal is a house that Mozart stayed in, a child—he was in Venice as part of his father's ambitions for him in European music. The high-arched bridge over the canal is being repaired and has plastic netting hiding one railing. Set into the placid water of the canal in an irregular perspective are workboats and reflections of façades. I am *in medias res,* in mid-sea, mid-drama, sailing in this double-comma-clawed city into one more day's new light. In this morning's piece of history, in this fragment of the history of the world, this narrow band of meandering water in the amphibious watery city is a pool of odors of moisture, night-damp and drying stones. The visual perfume of fragile sunlight touches the water and my mind which is sailing clumsily, disjointedly on its own voyages inside me. I am alone except for a few not very noisy seabirds and some silent, unchirping sparrows. . . . Ah, a street sweeper ahead of me, farther down the *calle,* starts to whistle; and a garbageman with his rubber-tired cart is active.

66   Around a curve and out of sight in this canal is the garbageman's moored barge, motor idling, waiting: I hear it now. I had not noticed the sound before, my own heart was so loud in me in the silence.

Comparisons have grown fewer. But how serious they are now. I am as old as the street sweeper but richer. I am older proportionately than Venice, closer to my death, but I am freer of violations.

(PF)

The light is in my eyes; I am squinting in strained, incredibly close, somewhat tearful attention beyond thought in the attention of memory. I am buried in the hasty other order of thought in giving and taking blows, *near tears,* tears of anger in the sunlight in the Piazza, in that other rage, in a fight, in the curious lost sense of having no other meaning but force, stamina, meanness, the brute astonishment of that, the *What does this mean?* when a blow unseated my balance or my mind—the pain, half-anesthetized—the pursed and jutting lips—the inwardly sucked and thinned lips—ah, Christ, the battered eyelids, the shattered nose and bruised chest, the erectile agony of fighting all out in a rush of hot blood and fear and will. . . .

Time plunges and glides, splashing me, drowning me, the fool-pacifist. . . . My moments are me, are my face, my arms. Like a boy I still live in the flutter and splash of overt time but I live now on the other side of my own history.

Venice! My body, my mind, and spirit veer in this morning's fever of remembering. I remember my phallic embarrassment, my covert readiness for the exigencies of rivalry, my startled—and partly *hysterical*–wish to escape invidious and insolent comparisons. In the melodramatic silence of the early hour, I walk crookedly and almost sightlessly and wake from that, sighing, and walk, alertly sauntering and staring. . . . *We had no time for courtship in* our *Venice. We were almost Protestant we were so quick, so abrupt.*

Through the colonnade, past shop windows I go and descend the three steps into, first, the shadow, then the sunlight in the empty Piazza. The glare struck me in the face, on the bones of the forehead and on the cheekbones. In a lagoon of glare, across the great, paved space in front of me rode San Marco. I found myself *squinting* as in a fistfight. How unrevised the bizarrely pretty façade of San Marco is, how comparatively uncorrected over eleven centuries. Never given a modern façade in any later period of the modern, untouched by any overall subsequent thought, an unrevised, *successful* idea, that long admired and accepted—it is disordering to someone alive in the moments.

And it is clothed in criminality. It wears the dress of stolen marbles and abducted sculptures. Clad in theft and pale in the early glare shortly after dawn, in the first sunshine of the day, there it is, standing in its sublime, inanimate confidence, in its lasting powers of seduction. . . . It was unendurable. What lingers in Venice is the track or wake of success embedded in the outspread architectural realities of the city. This is the surviving shell of an old criminal faith, a petrified and inlaid den of talented watchfulness.

Venice has no pagan roots. It is the primal city of Christian success.

I stood—victimized, martyred—in mood, you understand—captured by that millennium-old fragility, the disagreeably enrapturing quality of its sugary, entirely un-Roman beauty.

The early morning light glittered along the upflung marble foam of the diadems above the entrances and among the evangelists of the roofline. The dull copies of the marvelous Byzantine horses paced in shadow. I am tired of my religious fevers and of my terrors. I might even welcome death.

(PF)

It is yet another form of Venice, this death, this extraordinary island, this shrinking and expanding Venice of darkness and isolation and of self-judgment without air, the riches of the world receding . . . the world receding like a Zattere of distant lights, golden, with guitar and flute music audible across the water, and girls visible far away.

To die to the world as if in thought or as if in monastic contemplation, disentangled from political and cultural moments and *shudderingly* unguided, unguarded . . .

(PF)

I sit here and listen to my heart tick. Time here in Venice is an inconceivably smooth, if watery, caress, full, of course, of light and glimmers of motion. It is almost as warming as light, time here, where history dresses itself by day and night in pretty monuments, in monumental façades and stone figures of considerable grace in a city of such monuments, a city set into the water like a stone ship in a dream and lit by night and day in order to see and feel its own grace in chill winds and fog and in summer heat and spring lightness. The enduring cleverness of the endearments locked in fine cornices and handsome windows and well-made steps, the unending power of amusement of thought-out beauty and ratio grants an often severe delight, even to fools, even to me.

For the moment I regret nothing. For the moment. For this moment. I miss the old colors of the stones here, the colors of when I was young here, and the old sounds of people in the *calli* and on the *fondamenta,* the different footsteps and bustle, the old quality of local voices, and the busier and brighter-colored pigeons in the light of childhood, the sharper outcry of birds in the garden, the passage of boats along the Giudecca and the liners in their gigantic scale dwarfing the city, the awful smoke of the coal stoves, the numbers of children everywhere. . . . I regret the disappearance of my life.

In the Ca' Marinention where I sit and draw doodles on the last page of the manuscript of the book I came to Venice to write, in this window-to-everywhere-and-to-beauty that Venice is—and that the mind is—I see the wall across the *campo* and the restless leaves of the small trees in the *campo,* and the softly restless, reflection-stained green water of the *rio.* Above a sequence of roofs sunlight rests on the upper part of the campanile of the Frari.

I did not dare attempt a serious representation of Venice but tried only to hint at a small experience of love in this setting, in the marvelous water-shine and amoral sunlight of this place that is so dear to me. I did not dare to try to hint at the daily actuality of these islands, of these palaces and *campi* and the serious churches and the inhabitant paintings of the churches in their sometimes fearsome beauty. Instead, I drew on the city's centuries-old indulgence in the profane and its invention of secular grace.

(PF)

An Instruction

"It is Venice . . . lonely, old, trampled-on Venice. . . . Queen whore of the world . . . Strange . . . What is here flowers here. Nowhere else. It cannot be transplanted. . . . Such a trim, strange corner of the ocean . . . here was a city in which the lowest common denominator and brute human strength did not rule. Isn't that interesting?

"It is not a tragic story, it has no poetry—it is only a movie . . . that is to say, an arm of commercial enterprise, as the wily and pragmatic Venetians tried to make love itself. . . . Do you know that? As an industry, it didn't take up too much room on these crowded islands for the income it produced. The women were the com-

merce of the city, glowing breasts. And the paled, sated men. It is not a joke, not a tragedy.

"Wonderful, isn't it, success? Power and success are gorgeous things. But a bit mediocre if they do not become gorgeous. The Venetians of the Most Serene Republic were very clever about this mediocrity: they executed mediocre admirals, assuming treachery, since the admirals should have managed to be driven and inspired by love and fear and pride toward Venice to rise above themselves. . . . Do you see?"

Then: "The small-statured Venetians were like children riding on the ocean—think of them—think of admirals the size of children in those little suits of armor. Imagine them as little old men—in this Venice, around us—with their pictures and statues, their pages and slaves and local whores. They stayed alive differently from us. Only a few of the rich ones, of the rich Venetians married—did you know that? They kept the fortunes concentrated. The rich men, out of jealousy, made their wives wear high shoes, buskins, so high-soled and -heeled the women could not walk but only totter. They could not swiftly duck in anywhere. The grotesquery of the tall, tall tottering wives with their dyed yellow hair married to the short, brilliant, jealous men in this clear Venetian light . . . The grotesquery meant they were beloved—at least in this sense—in this pretty city. . . . The short High Admirals were rich and ruthless. . . . *Come live with me and be my love* but in this wind, tourists barefoot in the cold water; other tourists passing on temporary wooden bridges; clouds sailing overhead, the lights over the Piazza swinging in the wind . . . Was Venice a city of elopements as Shakespeare suggested? There was a surfeit, an overabundance of marriageable young women. They were put into convents where they misbehaved."

(PF)

Have you ever seen Venice from the air, a compact mass of buildings, carefully higgledy-piggledy with no area for the assembly or barracking of forces? Byzantium could never have used the lagoon as a substitute for Ravenna. The city is closer to the sea than to the mainland; it has no relation to armies. It rises behind the thin sand curl of the Lido, separated from the sea as if by an eyelid. In a small plane, the lagoon is a half hour's flight from end to end—this is an enormous space for a city-state. In the fourteenth century, Venice was as large in its way as Brazil is now. The waters of the lagoon are a mass of colors—green, pearly gray, dark gray, blue-gray, bits of sun glare. Venetian purple is visible in shadows, in colored swathes and tinted patches. The marsh shallows are sometimes rust-red. The water reflects the blue and gray of distances. And here and there are the greens of trees on various islets, different greens fluttering. And red-tile roofs . . . Until the 1600s, before the domes were built, the city was in outline somewhat like a marsh itself, like a marsh with reeds and grasses rising from the

76   water, the verticals of the nonwatery; and not floating; in
     Venice the verticals, as if of grasses, were buildings filled,
     crammed with lives; but rooted and grasslike; except for
     a few of the churches which rose high like tents or ships'
     hulls upside down in the air. Venetian love is problem-
     atic. Is it love if you do not love someone best?

                                                    (PF)

Notes on Venice

I have not been serious in my life. I have not seriously devoted myself to a cause. Or dedicated myself to an idea. My life has been largely in my keeping—a selfish, Venetian sort of life.

The unideal fantasy of Venice, the realized fantasies of wealth and amusement—of happy endings in a sense— are still visible, largely as architectural remains and economic murmurs and flutters of a still existent cosmopolitanism and marvelousness. (Think of the ways great cities ceaselessly advertise themselves as marvels

with towers and bus lines, subways and theaters, lights
and piazzas, crowds and viciousness; of the ways they
relate to distance and to topography and to light, Berlin
light, New York light, Paris light, the light in London.)
And then the reality of family life, of shouts, of kisses, of
a love affair, the announcement in the manifest physical
reality of beauty and pleasure, of carrying out fantasies
of the will—the pleasures of the mind being often no
more than an unphysical exercise of the will, as in building a city in the water or as in the transposition to wealth
(i.e., to money) or to ideas, the translation of everything,
a kind of universal, universally human, metaphor—so
here, in this wintry city in March, among the watery real
estate, one deals with the painfully evident fact that each
life is different.

Its dirty and expensive pleasures, and among them a
quick sick rivalry with Henry James and with Ruskin
that one cannot win. . . .

The wealth and comfort—and decadence and genuinely
wicked pleasures—of a city, of a compressed and walled
and magical city rising from a plain or on a plateau or
atop a hill or on an island, fortified, all of that is com-
pounded in Venice, which has been in its time austere
and pure, hard-living and hard-fighting, guileful, the
bank of Europe, the mind of Europe, the whorehouse of
Europe.

Money made it resonate; the fancifulness of it created the place, identified and seduced a population, seduced its loyalty.

Adriatic harshness and toughness, Thracian toughness, horses and men, Macedonia and mountains and valleys.

Most humane state: medicine, charity, religious tolerance (up to a point).

The curious set of gilded accidents that made Venice and which then dismantled her so that she herself, in her watery avatar, never has experienced the industrial age. Arabian Gothic and Renaissance geometrical and sinful city offering a fabric of walls. Roman, Greek. The intelligence of the place.

Two channels, one straight, one quite strongly curved. The handsome curve became the center of the water-walled city.

The original idea was safety. The interplay between safety and terror is an interesting one: what is the idea of safety or the reality of it if terror is not an issue and is not at issue at all times and strongly. The unanesthetized soul must be aware of the danger in the moments, of the limitlessness of danger, and of what is contained in danger, humiliation, failure, and extinction. . . . During its fourteen hundred years these things happened in fewer instances to Venetians abroad and in fewer instances in Venice itself than elsewhere in the world.

Venice. Attacked: assailed, assaulted, insulted, descried, denigrated, as if humiliated, defeated up to a point —surrounded by politicians and bribe takers and bribe givers, the angry low and the murderous and murmurous, the ill-intentioned illiterate, the savagely untalented.

Sexual safety—fucking in a pillaged city—Venetian pricks, Venetian cunts and breasts—and hair . . .

Venice
    The name in English is visually mimetic: the *V* suggests waves but is also the roof of a campanile or a Gothic

82   arch upside down; and the *e*'s and *n* and *c* suggest the Byzantine domes; and the *i*, the Gothic pier or the shaft of the campanile.

The movement of the water, the shifting of the globe as the earth spins in space . . .

(1992)

Lecture Notes

To begin this discussion, let us mention the unmendable relativism of reality. And then, before we speak of the men of proud mind of the Republic (we can only guess at the largely unrecorded women; the women were constrained by neighborhood and by cultural tactics) let us point out that the chief problem in education or in the formation of character is alternately the pain, the incredible stress that flexibility and openness impose on a competent, experienced self, and then the time that thought requires and which is never given us in sufficient quantity even if we go to live in the desert.

And then consider the fact of sailing, of mostly coastal sailing, and how it grants time to think, inter-

spersed with immediate action; and one begins to see the quality of mind and of strategy and of policy that was, for a thousand years, *Venetian*.

This quality of mind and of being translated to dry land tasks, such as publishing or governing, is also visibly Venetian. The public authority one must gain before anyone attends to what we say—what that was based on in Venice—and the oddity that that sort of thought and that having spent time thinking confers on a man and on a people in relation to their fellows.

And the time to read does not exist in Venice, and to check what others have to say depends on a sort of high journalism that is also one of the core elements in Venetian art, including architecture. To adopt and assimilate or oppose and reject or modify and tentatively use the ideas of merit proposed by such journalism is the central Venetian art.

(There is a sort of Venetian display in Paris and then in London. And think of Amsterdam's canals. . . .)

Such matters as canonical status do not exist in the Venetian context.

Montale (in reference to Auden in Venice overseeing the premiere of *The Rake's Progress*): I will never experience the joy of being a foreigner in Italy. God knows I've tried; but when you're born here, you haven't a chance.

Time and the canon. The canon has the primary aspect of suggesting a possible orderliness in ranking and respect. This has to do with one's use of time, at least culturally, as in choosing to study certain texts held in some sort of large-scale common regard—which is what canonical status is—but in Venice we have a splashier sense of order in the use of time, a watery nowness, an immediate functionality, a function in immediacy, the production of income, the mastery of power, a generic potency based on being the richest, the world summit. Nothing else so seizes the imagination.

A secondary aspect of canonical status is that once it has been conferred, such status changes the angle of argument. Venice has not been granted canonical status in the manner in which such status has been granted Florence and Rome, and London and Paris.

Catholic cities versus Protestant ones . . . The gorgeousness and the sinful quality.

I do not know what love is if it is not the motion of consciousness, the only motion and susceptibility consciousness has, and which we twist when we pretend to nonmotion. The motion of love. In life in the passage of time, in the great explosion that life is—in the one-way, nonstop accumulation of moments, moments and

88 notions and motions. *La dee da tra la la . . . tra la la . . .* love is all there is. But you can color it. A beach rat on the shore near Iesolo in the wind, a smallish animal loose in the day, in the mischievous light under flying clouds, in the obvious laws of simple flight. Simple fear perhaps loves life. It has a logic of the erotic, a violence of amorous alertness—the beast does. The beasts instruct the world.

(1993)

A Writer in Venice

Spring 1994
I am lying diagonally among twists of linen sheeting in
an enormous bed in a shuttered room under a giant
glass chandelier glimmering complicatedly. I am in an
apartment near San Tomà, with motionless white curtains masking the shuttered windows. I hear the war-
bles, coos, flutters of birds outside the shutters and the
sounds of the reconstruction of the Casa Goldoni. Workmen's shouts, children, a dog. I hear the fluffing rise and
shifting fall or slap of water in the small *rio* at the foot of
the building wall, my bedroom wall. The room shakes
lightly with the strange, pervasive vibrations of the traffic on the Grand Canal.

It is April and the start of my second year as an AIDS patient. I am in Venice at the invitation of Michael Naumann, my German publisher, to celebrate the release, in Germany, of my new novel, *Profane Friendship*. I am in Venice, but the sensation is that I wake in a box of consciousness of my own breath—without enthusiasm yet with wryly comic relief at not being dead, at not waking with a scream. I am very weak and fragile, and I find everything to be odd. Illness makes me shy; being ill is like the experience of public nakedness in dreams. In addition to AIDS, or in conjunction with it, I have bronchitis from the bad air on the plane during the flight here. Venice has been rainy and cold, and then hot; when I go out, I hear coughing all over the city.

10:15 A.M. My friend Giovanni Alliata-Cini's gesture in the *calle*, when we unexpectedly meet: he takes my hand in both of his and holds it and warms it. A deeply affecting death knell.

10:45 A.M. At a *traghetto* landing, in extraordinary, uncontaminated, assaultive light, as bright as if the sky held tiny particles of sharp-edged, gleaming glass, a bright, transparent glass dust. In this cutting light, the colors of the gardens and the colors of the buildings and the water in the Grand Canal do not disappear in glare or grow pale but take on a weird practical aura of being dressed up, brushed, and polished—the very distances in the view are polished. But not in the shade. There the water is dull, dirtyish, dark gray-green, and the stones show every crack. The dressed-up quality and the run-down quality observed together create an atmosphere of intimacy—perhaps one should say an extremely intimate reality.

Out on the choppy Canalazzo, among the vaporetti and scows and barges and the pretty *motoscafi*, the black ferries, called *traghetti*–which are rather plump open gondolas without seats, with one boatman at the bow and one at the stern poling twistingly and much more quickly than the regular *gondolieri* do—carry their erect, lightly swaying passengers standing very close to one another. Dressed in business clothes and carrying briefcases or portfolios; or in jeans and carrying schoolbooks; or in proper skirts and blouses, bearing string bags of vegetables and flowers in rolls of paper; or in work clothes, with tools in their arms or boxes balanced on their heads—these figures in a silent, polite clump are carried in the crowded craft over the water and its heaving reflections. It is very pictorial, a mystery of city existence, those lives swaying in the dark boat against a backdrop of palazzi and water traffic.

Six or seven Frenchmen and women of modest demeanor—not young, not well-dressed—came briskly along the *calle,* pushing wheelchairs in which were youngish, twisted-up people, two of them breathing loudly and presenting distorted faces and looking enraged and/or sullen. A third, with a lifted clawlike hand, looked murderous. But the look was a viewer's misapprehension about retardation and deformity— about something childlike and perhaps truly innocent, although a real rage may have been there. They all seemed caged in special virtue, in special suffering, morally irresistible. (One time, driving through Indiana, my wife, Ellen, and I came upon a town that had a locally famous institution for people who required special care. These people worked around the town in stores and gas stations, and everyone adjusted to them. An ordinary townsman told me that it had once been a religious town but no longer trusted religion—because of Vietnam, he said. The townspeople had apparently replaced religion with devotion to the goodness and suffering of the slightly mad, the ill-since-birth, and the retarded. Everyone in the town seemed to me incontrovertibly good.)

This *traghetto* landing is not far from the railroad station. Often, as soon as people disembark here, they break into an all-out run up the narrow *calle*.

A *traghetto* is efficient and rides lightly on the water but is not stable, and it costs only five hundred lire, or a third of a dollar—the cheapest form of gondola ride in the city. Wind among the tallish palazzi adds swirls to the current and to traffic-churned waves and blows on the clumped people as on a clumsy sail. An anemometer whirls atop a metal rod on the dock. I have seen people in wheelchairs on *traghetti* but only one at a time and only ordinary people, not those caged in specialness: I have seen the *traghetto* men take a folded wheelchair and unfold it on the *traghetto* while an ill man hobbled into the boat on his wife's arm and then sat in the chair, the wind blowing his hair while he held his hat in his lap.

The *traghetto* men are mostly polite but standoffish, except toward one another; they display their warmth and solidity and amusement with one another. They are not forward like *gondolieri,* at least in my experience. They prefer not to be helpful. But sometimes they are. I have never seen one of them address a woman on the boat itself, but I have seen them be forward in the *calli* and in the bars. They inherit their rights to the *traghetto* crossing. They are as independent-seeming as Charon or as ranchers in American Westerns. They take frequent breaks, so seven or eight of them work here, keeping two *traghetti* in motion throughout the day.

The French pushed the wheelchairs into a tangle among those waiting for the *traghetto* and those disembarking from one—that is, they expected to board as a matter of course. One of the younger *traghetto* men waved them away. The *traghetto* men drink from morning on; they hold it well; but they are freed inside their daylong drunkenness. They are windblown and sunstruck, moderately tired, and somewhat drunk.

The oldest *traghetto* man, probably my age, showed his stolen and controlled drunkenness more than the younger men did. He hurried over to the French to get them out of the way. I doubt that he spoke to the point: he was allusive, artful, charming, intimate. One of the guardians, a woman, gave an affronted cry, a gull-like cry of argument, of reproach. The French, the guardians of the angelic crippled, were stiff with rebuke at his heartlessness. He was pointing down the canal, to where, twenty-five yards away (though you would have to walk inland and then out to the canal again to reach it), there was a vaporetto stop. (Such stops have ramps, and each vaporetto has a central open space, where you often see people in wheelchairs.) During this episode, my own physical weakness caused me to unfocus and refocus. Also, there was the wind, and the space between me and the French. The perpetual children in the wheelchairs were caught in currents of thighs and mid-sections as foot traffic moved toward the boats or inland. The French were blocking most of the passage. The Italians dexterously wriggled past while accepting the circumstances of the others' being there, of there being a difficulty.

The French, observing the reality, lined the wheelchairs next to a railing on this portion of the *calle cum fondamenta*. This maneuver was performed with great deftness. There they stayed, forming a bank and narrowing the passage for perhaps ten minutes, until the guardians abruptly set off single file, pushing the chairs, heading inland like a line of cavalry, moving very quickly away from this submetaphysical corner of un-universal Venice.

11:10 A.M. Talk. Gossip. Conversation. In a hired boat. In our conferred stardom, out on the broad canal in the lightly explosive light, we experience illumination itself, but it is blinding and private: vision becomes recessive. The eyes recede under the brows, behind one's sunglasses, making one a sun dweller, an Italian, of a kind.

Ellen and I tell our friend Naumann about the French and the wheelchairs. We sit forward in the white *moto-scafo,* near the boatman, who has a degree of pallor and the worn skin of a mainland Venetian working only part-time in Venice, outdoors. We enter the city's eccentric, expensive water labyrinth. Now we are a point of focus, an element in the sub-immortal picture. People filing into a *traghetto* look at us as do those on a full vaporetto and those at windows in the palazzi, or on the stone banks of the canal. We talk and chug past the lovely and worn and irregular jumble of decorative windows and columns and stones and marble ornament—we ruffle the green, restless mirror of the water. The Istrian stone of the city shines in this light. Architectural patterns tower around us in the beautiful Venetian visibility. Venice seems to be only its surviving beauty, such as it now is, a structure of appearances without a secret reality. . . . Of course, it still has secrets, but they are minor ones. I cannot recall a conversation in Venice that did not start with the topic of Venice. Or, one, this trip, in which the next remarks were not about my having AIDS. Then about Ellen's health. And state of mind. Then . . . but modern conversation—even when shouted over the noise of the motor in bright sunlight, with the boat chauffeur standing there—has a curious quality of occurring in a parenthesis that will be lost inside the machinery of any attempted biography or replication.

In Berlin and Paris and New York and Milan, the gossip and news-giving go on by phone and fax every morning—exchanging the real stories of everything. And at dinners. At lunch. In private conversation, face-to-face, this is merely a form of intimacy, trust, respect of a kind.

But, as public statements, the remarks, the voices, become scabrous. Naumann and Ellen and I *talk;* we use our actual opinions, our best information—real stories about Venice, New York, Berlin. But the real story of my death, the real nature of Ellen's and my relationship is private, is not to be historicized, not to be noted. Not yet.

History is a scandal, as are life and death.

I am dying. . . . Venice is dying. . . . The century is dying. . . . The imbecile certitudes of the last three-quarters-century are dying. The best journalism of the last half-century has been leftist; which means that human nature was shown as innocent, as decent at the beginning and end of each story. A phantasmagoria, a piety, that idea—an abdication of reality, an infinite condescension toward anything less than absolute power. Similarly, novels were fantastic—like spaceships that as a matter of course left this world. The real was forbidden.

Our boatman did not at first remember San Sebastiano, the parish church of Veronese, but he accepted my description, spoken in a gasping baby's Italian. He half remembered then. For fifteen years, Veronese painted in that small church. He grew wise, so to speak—an aging mixture of cold and hot. We turned from the brilliant sunlight and the restless water of the Grand Canal into the shadow of a smaller canal leading to the Giudecca. I feel unwell restlessly, resentfully. Just before we turn into the wide Giudecca, I look up and see the people there on the *fondamenta* as taller than they are and foreshortened, like figures in a ceiling fresco. One group of young men, each of them oversized in a shapeless fashion—not exercised-looking, but strong, rough-haired, and loud, in tight clothes—were pushing and shouldering their way along, drinking as they strutted, and photographing themselves with a video camera. Fini people, the boatman said, Fascists.

We pulled out into the Giudecca, and they shrank in the distance. The current Italian Fascists are not quite *neo*-Fascists, as they claim; they are forced by Italian law to deny any connection to Mussolinian doctrines and deeds, but Mussolini's granddaughter is one of the leaders of their party. Not out in the *calli* but at the soccer stadium, in that national privacy, they shout anti-Semitic slogans and wave anti-Semitic placards. Apparently, it is possible to attend a game safely only if you sit on the expensive side of the stadium—as in England. Violence is the will of the people.

From the center of the Giudecca, across the water, in a distant haze, refineries and industrial chimneys on the heavily built-up mainland are visible. The industrial plant is outdated and no longer represents much in the way of money. It represents votes and redundant and unhappy workers. The local megalopolis stretches to the head of the Adriatic and around as far as Trieste. In the other direction, it runs through Padua and on to Mantua. Trieste and the Veneto and Venice and these other districts all together make up an urban conglomeration like the one around San Francisco Bay and down the peninsula.

The day smells of salt and sun and of the onset of blood. But Venice itself, in its watery surround, is parenthetical to immediate violence. The guardians of the churches and other places we visited demonstrated degrees of seduction and difficulty of temper toward foreigners. One, a usually very quiet man—Ellen and I see him frequently when we are in Venice—was in a state of explosive rage because someone had spilled Coca-Cola on a marble floor *nella chiesa,* "in the church." But it was not a consecrated church; it was the chapel of San Giorgio degli Schiavoni—St. George of the Slavs. Violence is the will of the people, off and on, and Venice was always racist.

8:00 P.M. Dinner at the Monaco, on the raft-terrace, sunset striping the sky with softly hazed bands of sulfur-polluted yellows and stained pinks and grayish mauves. The two domes of the Salute were backlit. The Dogana gleamed. The factories, the activities in Mestre and Santa Margherita, the flames of the refineries had been visible from the boat earlier, but the wind rather delicately carried a touch of pollution, chemical nastiness. The winds blew it here lightly, strange acidic elements in the Venice mixture of curling cool-and-damp and the African hot-and-dry. Boats crossing the Bacino were beginning to turn on their lights. Year by year, there is less variety among the boats. Venice, as it ages into being a museum of itself, grows simpler. But it is unlikely it can ever have the quality of true simplicity. It is elaboration itself. How I wish for the causeway and the railway to be dismantled, and for Venice to be cut off from the mainland and the lagoon restored to swamp, for the city's filled-in and paved canals to be returned to water, for Venice to be unpedestrian, isolated, impractical, wholly itself and unlike the rest of the world.

At the large table on the raft-terrace sit Naumann and Ellen and Fritz Raddatz, a critic for *Die Zeit,* who has admired my new novel in his column. A Berliner by birth, he now lives in Hamburg, and is here in Venice so that we can meet. He is en route to give a speech and a seminar in Rome. My German translator, Angela Praesent, who lives in southern France, is here, and Volker Hage, of *Der Spiegel,* is here; he is a model figure of the New Germany. Francesca De Pol, a Venetian, who works for the Consorzio Venezia Nuova, is here.

I may be the central figure of the dinner, but everywhere in the world—even in Paris—condescension flows from critics toward writers; the point of the critic is to demonstrate mastery in the contemporary moment. He or she has an army of readers, phalanxes literally. But a writer is alone, is a sacrificed beast and madman (or madwoman) and fool. Or is someone dying or drunken. This condescension is sometimes delicately or heavily lightened by admiration. Or by envy and rage. Or by sympathy. But a writer has no legions, no phalanxes in a direct sense, only a "name," a perfume, a reputation.

As the light around us altered, as shadows and glare played idly and jeeringly erased vast stretches of famous cityscape, Raddatz addressed me as *cher maître* in a tone that meant we were celebrating a private success, one that hadn't happened publicly yet, that might not happen. (Some books emerge as significant only over time and exist uneasily in the present moment as intellectual and political and economic facts. One can avoid this, can write differently.)

Raddatz is a man my age and has great energy—German energy, unlike American or Italian vigor, Böhm, as opposed to Bernstein or Giulini. I have never been energetic or active—strong, yes, at one time, but never adventurous or quick. Sitting in a chair on a raft-terrace is my sort of adventure. It is odd to me how aesthetic intelligence and a sense of—what to call it—journalistic and immediate power can seem grotesque with bravery and self-assertion, a madness of the normal, of normalcy.

Still, one might say at the table, among the people there, women and men—including the maître d' overseeing everything and present as well—that blind surges of power disordered the moments; reputations and imputed events and events-to-come quivered and rippled foreignly like the surfaces of the moving and darkening water at our feet. Power and the mix of cultures and genders and private stories were tactfully shaped in my favor—perhaps out of pity, perhaps out of respect.

One hardly expects *truth* anymore in anything, and Venice is, in any case, a city in which truth was used with a degree of fantasy to achieve a potent and salable insobriety—so human. It is a monument to fantasy-made-actual, insolently pictorial and mostly festive, self-hypnotically.

I will not attempt to do the voices or judge the talk or the moods on the raft-terrace.

It grew darker, and across the flickering water the lights bloomed on the façade of Palladio's Redentore. That Palladian façade has as an aesthetic quality, an un-Venetian and as-if-final, brooding stillness. It was built to honor the end of a plague. It testifies also to the wretched capitalism of the survivors—the city was already dying then; the façade is something of a tomb-stone for accident and evil, for ruin and death as if they will not occur again. . . .

I can't remember ever wishing life and death had a perceptible, known, overall meaning. When I was a child, I wished only for life, a little more of it, or much more of it. In the first torments of adolescence, I wished for a little less of it, for peace from it and its dangers. I think of breath as noisy and containing a kind of reason or meaning, as in the half-prayer of *Let me breathe*. I think of the mind as rebellious and made of interrup-tions and demands for the ideal and private flights; it is dangerous to love minds, even one's own. I have accepted since childhood the transience of everything, including meaning—poor orphan that I was. The arrival and departure of significance was something I was used to, not in the sense that the significance appears once and disappears for good, but in the sense that impure versions of it recur, as my party-loving parents came and went, dressed and left the house and returned: they return in memory still. This hasn't changed with illness. Death has a transient significance for me, one that changes. My sense of it changes, too—the imagery, the shock along the nerves, the fear (or terror) behind the breastbone. I tend to treat myself as if I were a nervous dog, a schnauzer, say. *It's all right*, I say to myself, *It's all right*. Sometimes it seems to me my blood, my bones, my nerves, my mind, my heart whisper to one another but not to me: I feel like the dissolving parent of the parts of me that there are. I would like to endow a small *chiesa* in Venice, to be called the Church of St. Death and the Ease of Leaving True Meaning Behind.

At some point, the waiters cranked out a brown-and-white striped awning, so that we were in a canvas-topped room beside the water. Some kinds of frivolity, like some kinds of selfish insistence, have an earnestness, a hidden skeleton of grace—I do not really understand this.

By ten-thirty I was exhausted, and, too tired for a *motoscafo*, I went with Ellen onto a vaporetto. We entered the cube of its lights. The vaporetto in a small surround of bright water in the middle of the dark held the casual fellowship of a public vehicle at night. It chug-chugged up the Canalazzo. I leaned on Ellen, who supported my weight as we went riding past the darkened or lit façades of the palaces of the Grand Canal.

(This Wild Darkness)

EDITOR'S NOTE

"To leave the surfaces of the world," Harold Brodkey wrote in a draft of his 1994 novel, *Profane Friendship*, "to abandon real *calli* and *fondamenta* for the Asias and Venices and seas in one's own head, is an old man's adventure." It is precisely this process of abstraction that made each successive draft of that novel more diaphanous and ethereal. With each revised version of the manuscript, any remaining trace of the actual Venice threatened to recede ever further into the mists that hover over the lagoon—or so it seemed to those of us who witnessed the creation and transformation of Brodkey's manuscript. The text appeared to us—his friends, editors, and translators—to forfeit literalness as it gained in spirituality.

My Venice arose from our resistance to the innumerable revisions, deletions, and expansions of *Profane Friendship* that the author made as he carried out his larger vision for the novel. A plan was devised to preserve the extended descriptions of Venice that Brodkey sacrificed for the sake of the novel's overall composition. The idea was to combine those passages with Brodkey's other writings on Venice, including early essays and lecture notes, and publish them in a single volume. At the heart of the project lay not philological or scholarly zeal but the fear that this material would otherwise be lost to posterity.

The text of *My Venice* presents the reader with a remarkably different Venetian cityscape from the one that appears in *Profane Friendship*. Although Brodkey ended up deleting only very few of his Venice reflections, in nearly every case he revised or repositioned them. Brodkey's poetics, his idiosyncratic and synesthetic manner of thinking—and seeing—come into focus in this volume as if through a zoom lens; we see his literary sleights of hand, as well as the deftness with which he moves between levels of reality and perception.

Brodkey's Venice is a spiritual and metaphoric one. "Venice was a subtrahend, a batch of negatives," he wrote. "It was not grim, not stern, not-a-lot-of-those-things. . . . And that added up to happiness, or to something like it." Although the author's Venice is often

constructed of negations, it does not collapse upon itself;
it is the ideal screen for Brodkey's paradoxical, time-
ridden psychological worldview. It recalls not the actual,
museumlike island city but those mental maps used by
professors of rhetoric to teach the memorization of com-
plex subjects. Brodkey's mnemonic map of Venice has
an additional dimension, however: it charts time as well
as space. "All of Venice has faded and been rebuilt brick
by brick in my lifetime," he writes. "I can date my life
and identify the years in which I had certain feelings by
the colors of the walls in my memory. . . ."

With each concrete image or social observation he
makes, Brodkey renders a philosophical or political
judgment. An offhand comment about Venice is also a
comment on the ever-changing not-Venice; on Rome;
on Catholic and Fascist Italy; on the United States; on
Puritanism; on socialism; on various absolutist doctrines; on un-Venetian tragedy, eroticism, metaphysics,
or aesthetics. Brodkey sometimes defines a phenome-
non, a person, a class, a city, by enumerating what it *isn't,*
or isn't any longer; he uncovers the thing itself.

One may believe—as Brodkey himself sometimes
did—that our capacity to perceive form and determine
place depends upon our ability to recognize contrast, to
compare the foreground to the background. But the
changes in Brodkey's texts come so swiftly, so manically,
that in the blink of an eye a single frame of reference
(whether historical, ontological, geopolitical, ideologi-
cal, or biographical) will transform into another, and

then another, all of them becoming inextricably tangled. Reading Brodkey can be a frightening—albeit fascinating—experience.

Brodkey's Venice. The mnemonic Venice. The Venice of dream and ecstasy, the rational, calculating Venice. Venice, with its billions of views and interpretations. "Venice and Venetian culture and eroticism had the charm of continuous safety over centuries; there is room for personal extravagance," he wrote.

In the spring of 1992, Harold Brodkey traveled to Venice on the invitation of Consorzio Venezia Nuova, a government-funded cultural foundation. He quickly adopted the role of the privileged outsider, with its endless opportunities for subtle witticism. Brodkey had once written that "Venice was never literary," since "it could not supply the necessary loneliness"; nevertheless, he began to write—a great deal and with great speed.

The Consorzio asked for nothing more from its guest author than an elegant essay inspired by Venice, much as the previous Fellows, the poet Joseph Brodsky and the cultural historians André Chastal and Giuseppe Sinopoli, had produced.

Ironically, in the wake of the cool American reception of *The Runaway Soul*, Brodkey responded to this request with a surge of creative output. Over the course of ten months, he wrote a novel that ran to more than four hundred pages. That novel, titled *Profane Friend-*

ship, was immediately translated into Italian and published privately by the Consorzio. In a *New Yorker* piece published in February 1994, nearly a year after his diagnosis with the AIDS virus, Brodkey wrote, "I had written a novel in one year, a novel that I liked, that I was proud of, and I had expected such a labor to kill me."

Several motifs are easy to detect in this collection: an implicit dialogue with the Victorian art historian and Venice connoisseur John Ruskin; the effect that Venice's unique economic, political, and religious situation has had on the historical mentality of its people; and a concern that runs through all of Brodkey's work—the "unrepeatable singularity" of time.

To Brodkey, Venice, which he calls "the most human of all cities," is not one of the canonized cities, such as Paris and London. Accordingly, citizens of Venice have never felt constrained by a fixed set of beliefs, an attitude that has helped the local imagination to flourish. Significantly, Brodkey adopted a city of the un-absolute as his spiritual homeland.

What is equally remarkable is that Brodkey identified closely with the city itself. Some of his notes can be viewed not merely as sketches of Venetian history, but also as a self-portrait of the artist. "Attacked: assailed, assaulted, insulted, descried, denigrated, as if humiliated, defeated up to a point—surrounded by politicians and bribe takers and bribe givers, the angry low and the murderous and murmurous, the ill-intentioned illiterate, the savagely untalented." Venice, where a happy ending can be wrested from simply "the avoidance of bankruptcy or tragedy." In Venice, Brodkey described himself—and the present condition of literature—as an economically obsolete object of wonder, historically estranged from the mainstream.

Harold Brodkey evokes Venice as a state of mind; as a premonition of what might remain were Europe's ancient hatreds finally quelled; as an imaginary place where to live in the moment need not preclude an awareness of history. Venice is at once bourgeois and bohemian, patrician and plebeian, democratic and elitist; a place that is driven by lust and industry, a city both rational and mad, where even safety is full of peril, and where pragmatism blends with the yearning for far-off places, while idealism remains defiantly local.

For those who enjoy such paradoxes, Brodkey's Venice is a natural meeting place. Brodkey wrote in 1994 that he "would like to endow a small *chiesa* in Venice, to be called the Church of St. Death and the Ease of Leaving True Meaning Behind." Under Brodkey's radical vision, Venice collapses into a primordial Venice: "How I wish for the causeway and the railway to be dismantled," he wrote, "and for Venice to be cut off from the mainland and the lagoon restored to swamp, for the city's filled-in and paved canals to be returned to water, for Venice to be unpedestrian, isolated, impractical, wholly itself and unlike the rest of the world."

What Brodkey has given us is a free-floating, self- contradictory Venice. It falls to the reader to locate the author's own Venice in the midst of all the other Venices, without actually having to visit Brodkey's little *chiesa*.

–Angela Praesent
Cotignac, France
July 1997

(Translated from the German by Elizabeth Gaffney)

Photographs by Giuseppe Bruno,
printed by permission of Biblos srl.

Excerpts from *Profane Friendship* by Harold Brodkey copyright © 1994 by Harold Brodkey. Reprinted by permission of Farrar, Straus & Giroux, Inc.

"On the Waves" from *Stories in an Almost Classical Mode* by Harold Brodkey copyright © 1988 by Harold Brodkey. Reprinted by permission of Alfred A. Knopf, Inc.

Excerpts from *This Wild Darkness: The Story of My Death* by Harold Brodkey copyright © 1996 by the Estate of Harold Brodkey. Reprinted by permission of Henry Holt and Company, Inc.